Must Know 100 Facts about the Animal Life

Om Books International

First Published in 2025 by

Om Books International

Corporate & Editorial Office
A-12, Sector 64, Noida 201 301
Uttar Pradesh, India
Phone: +91 120 477 4100
Email: editorial@ombooks.com
Website: www.ombooksinternational.com

Sales Office
107, Ansari Road, Darya Ganj
New Delhi 110 002, India
Phone: +91 11 4000 9000
Email: sales@ombooks.com
Website: www.ombooks.com

ISBN: 978-93-52761-82-1

Printed in India

10 9 8 7 6 5 4 3 2 1

CONTENTS

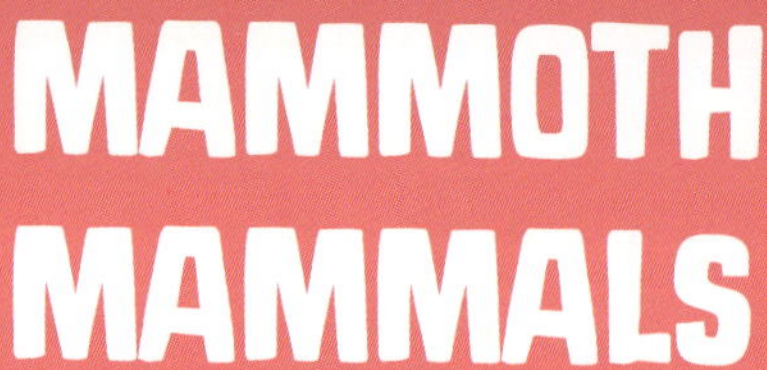

MAMMOTH MAMMALS

Fun Fact

Did you know that a group of zebras is called a dazzle? This name highlights their unique striped patterns. It confuses predators and helps keep them safe.

BLUE WHALE: BEHEMOTH OF THE OCEAN

The blue whale is the largest animal known to have ever existed. It can grow up to 30 metres (98 feet) in length and weigh as much as 150 tonnes. These marine giants survive mainly on tiny krill, consuming about 4 tons of it each day.

GIANTS OF THE LAND: AFRICAN ELEPHANTS

The African elephant is the largest land animal on Earth, with adult males weighing up to 6,350 kilograms (14,000 lbs). These massive mammals are distinguished not just by their size but by their large ears. These help to regulate their body temperature in the hot African climate.

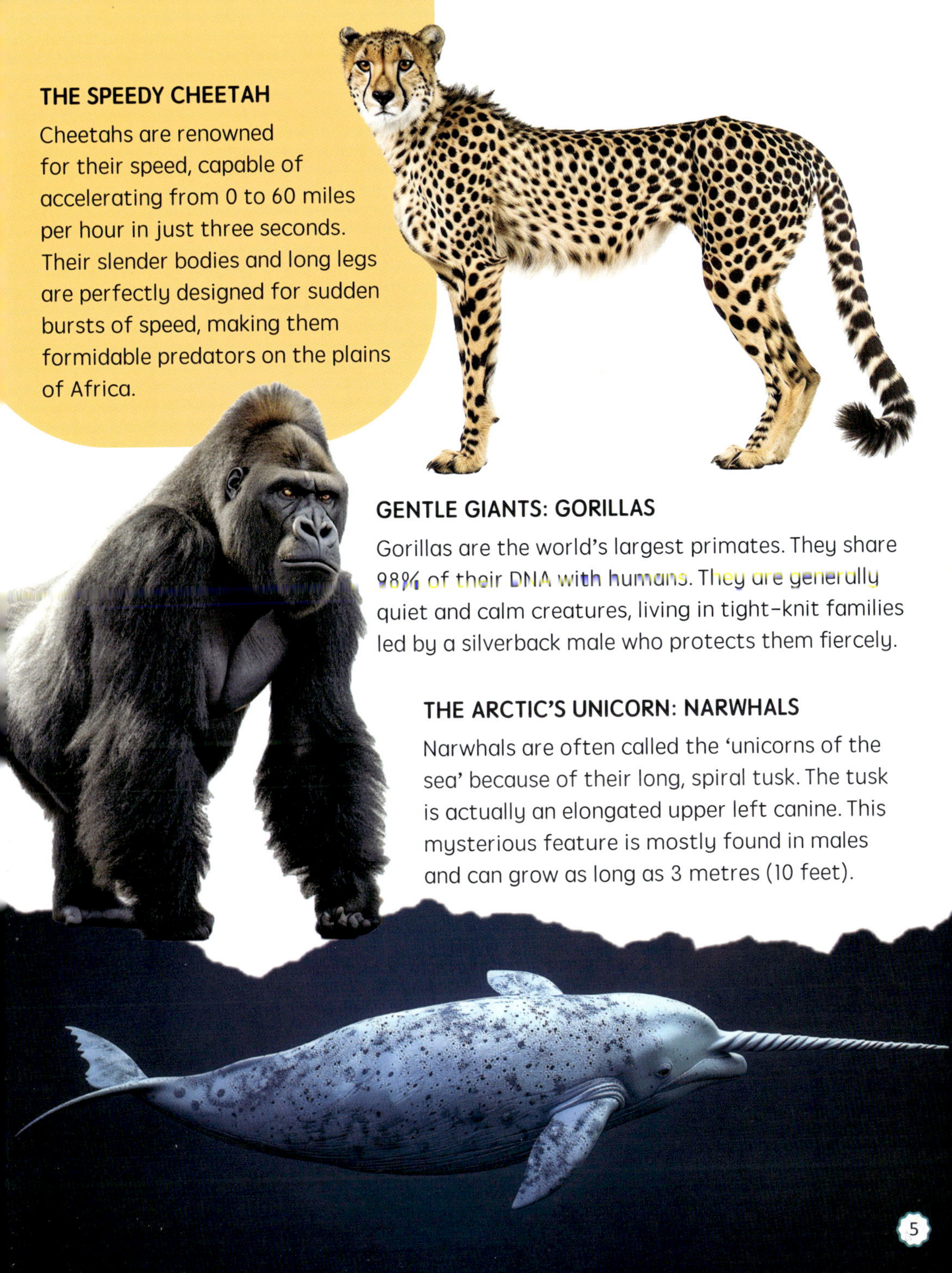

THE SPEEDY CHEETAH

Cheetahs are renowned for their speed, capable of accelerating from 0 to 60 miles per hour in just three seconds. Their slender bodies and long legs are perfectly designed for sudden bursts of speed, making them formidable predators on the plains of Africa.

GENTLE GIANTS: GORILLAS

Gorillas are the world's largest primates. They share 98% of their DNA with humans. They are generally quiet and calm creatures, living in tight-knit families led by a silverback male who protects them fiercely.

THE ARCTIC'S UNICORN: NARWHALS

Narwhals are often called the 'unicorns of the sea' because of their long, spiral tusk. The tusk is actually an elongated upper left canine. This mysterious feature is mostly found in males and can grow as long as 3 metres (10 feet).

FEATHERED FRIENDS

HUMMINGBIRD HUSTLE

Hummingbirds are the only birds that can fly backwards. Their wings can beat up to 80 times per second. Their heart rate can reach more than 1,260 beats per minute, supporting their high-speed aerial antics.

PENGUINS: TUXEDOS IN THE COLD

While penguins might waddle awkwardly on land, they are graceful swimmers. Their black and white plumage offers camouflage while swimming. The white undersides blend with the bright surface water, and the dark backs with the ocean depths.

Fun Fact

A flamingo's pink colour comes from the beta carotene in the aquatic organisms that they eat. The more they consume, the pinker they become!

WISE OLD OWLS

Owls are known for their exceptional night vision. They can turn their heads as much as 270 degrees. This ability allows them to see in almost any direction without moving their bodies.

KING OF THE SKIES: THE BALD EAGLE

The bald eagle, a symbol of strength and freedom, boasts a wingspan of up to 8 feet. It can fly at altitudes of 10,000 feet. They use their powerful vision to spot prey from great distances.

THE MAJESTIC PEACOCK

Peacocks are famous for their spectacular tail feathers, which they fan out to attract females. These feathers feature eye-like designs that shimmer in the sunlight.

REPTILIAN WONDERS

AGELESS ALLIGATORS

Despite their bulky appearance, alligators are surprisingly fast. They are capable of sprinting at speeds of up to 35 miles per hour, which is faster than most humans. However, they lack the stamina for sustained high-speed movement.

Fun Fact

The leatherback sea turtle can dive to depths of approximately 4,000 feet, deeper than any other turtle, and can stay submerged for up to 85 minutes.

THE MIGHTY ANACONDA

The green anaconda is the heaviest snake in the world. It is capable of growing up to 9 metres (30 feet) long and weighing as much as 227 kilograms (550 pounds). They are powerful swimmers and often lurk in the rivers of South America.

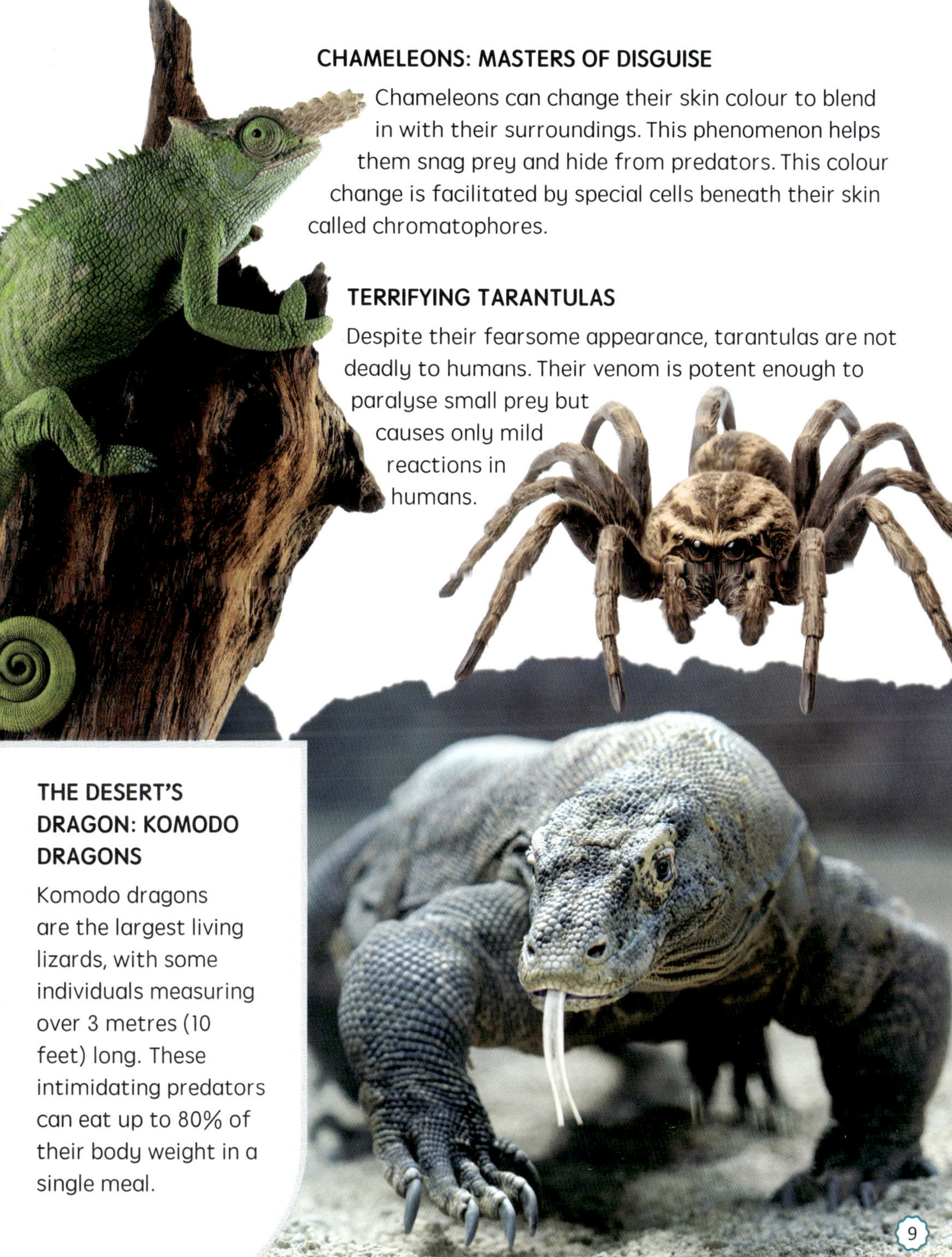

CHAMELEONS: MASTERS OF DISGUISE

Chameleons can change their skin colour to blend in with their surroundings. This phenomenon helps them snag prey and hide from predators. This colour change is facilitated by special cells beneath their skin called chromatophores.

TERRIFYING TARANTULAS

Despite their fearsome appearance, tarantulas are not deadly to humans. Their venom is potent enough to paralyse small prey but causes only mild reactions in humans.

THE DESERT'S DRAGON: KOMODO DRAGONS

Komodo dragons are the largest living lizards, with some individuals measuring over 3 metres (10 feet) long. These intimidating predators can eat up to 80% of their body weight in a single meal.

BUGS AND BEETLES

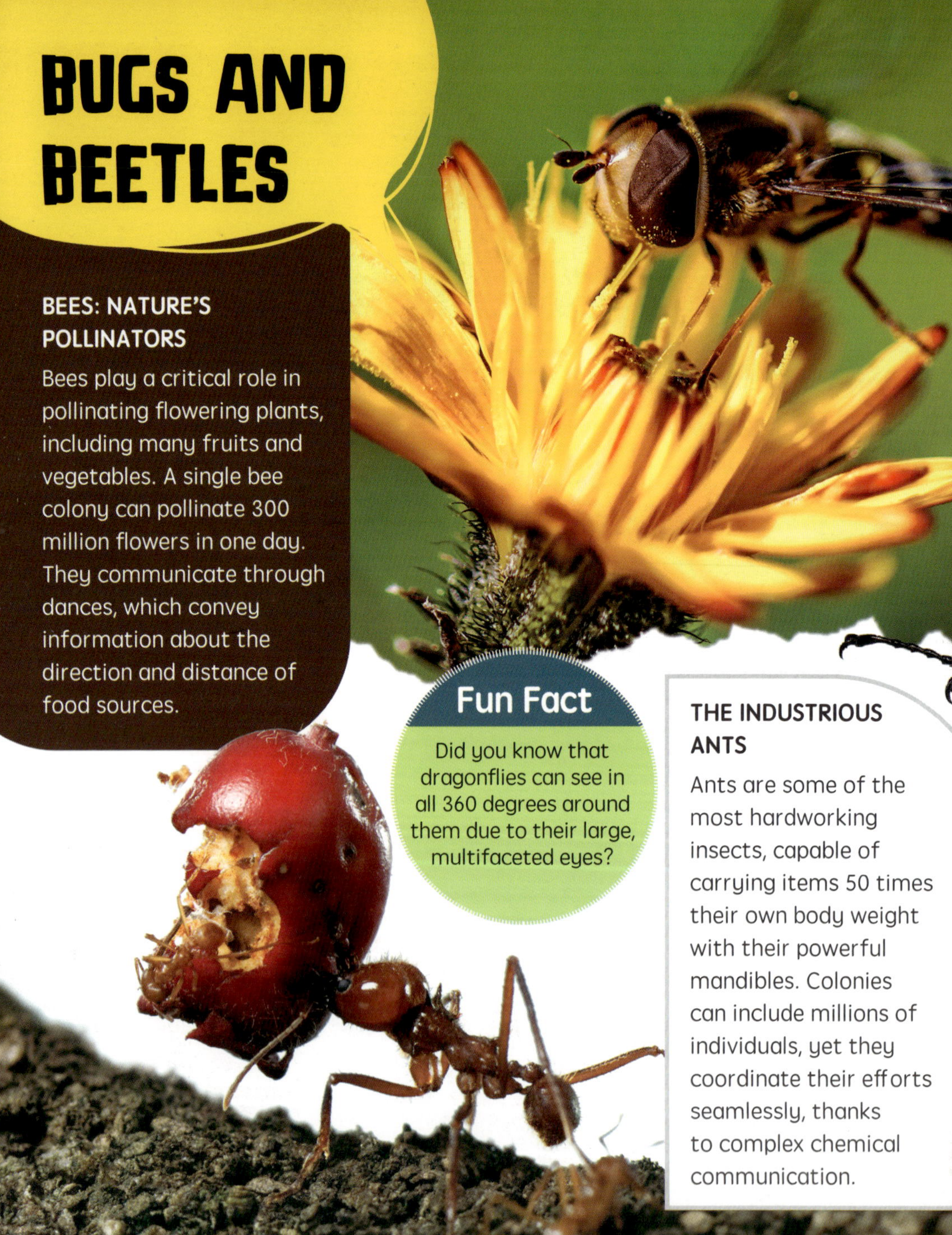

BEES: NATURE'S POLLINATORS

Bees play a critical role in pollinating flowering plants, including many fruits and vegetables. A single bee colony can pollinate 300 million flowers in one day. They communicate through dances, which convey information about the direction and distance of food sources.

Fun Fact

Did you know that dragonflies can see in all 360 degrees around them due to their large, multifaceted eyes?

THE INDUSTRIOUS ANTS

Ants are some of the most hardworking insects, capable of carrying items 50 times their own body weight with their powerful mandibles. Colonies can include millions of individuals, yet they coordinate their efforts seamlessly, thanks to complex chemical communication.

THE LUMINOUS FIREFLIES

Fireflies are famous for their bioluminescence. They produce light through a chemical reaction that occurs in their abdomens called luciferases. This light is used for mating signals.

THE MIGHTY HERCULES BEETLE

The Hercules beetle is one of the largest beetles. It is capable of growing up to 19 centimetres long. The horn is used in battles with other males over territory and mates, remarkably lifting or flipping their rivals.

THE ARCHITECTURAL WONDERS OF SPIDER WEBS

Spiders use their silk to create intricate webs that serve as both their hunting grounds and homes. The silk is strong. Spiders use it to float, attaching to other surfaces to expand their territory.

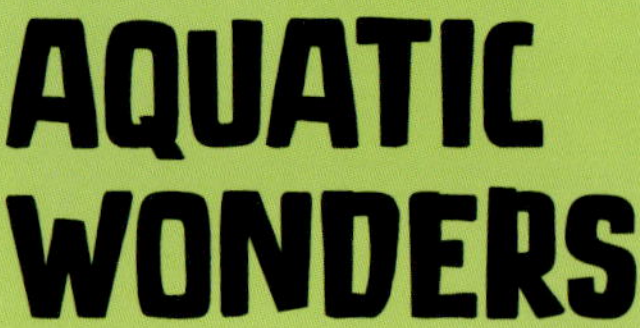

AQUATIC WONDERS

Fun Fact

Starfish can regrow their arms if they are damaged or severed. In some species, an entire new starfish can grow from a single severed limb.

THE MYSTERIOUS GIANT SQUID

Giant squids are deep-ocean dwelling. They can grow to a tremendous size, potentially up to 13 metres (43 feet) long. They are known for their large eyes, which are as big as soccer balls, to help them see in the murky depths.

INTELLIGENT DOLPHINS

Dolphins are highly intelligent and social animals. They have been known to use tools to communicate complex ideas through various sounds. They display behaviours that suggest a high level of emotional intelligence.

THE COLOURFUL CLOWNFISH

Clownfish are brightly coloured fish famous for their symbiotic relationship with sea anemones. They are immune to the anemone's stings. They hide from predators within their tentacles while keeping the anemone clean and free from parasites.

SEAHORSES: TINY OCEAN CURIOSITIES

Beyond their unique shape, seahorses are known for males carrying and birthing their offspring. Capable of colour change, they also possess prehensile tails that wrap around stationary objects. The tail secures them in flowing waters.

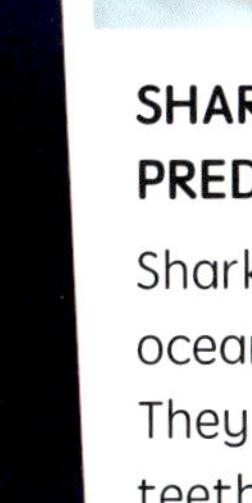

SHARKS: THE OCEAN'S TOP PREDATOR

Sharks have roamed the world's oceans for over 400 million years. They have multiple rows of sharp teeth that can be replaced within a day if they lose one.

THE SKY'S LIMIT

THE HIGH-FLYING ALBATROSS

The albatross is renowned for having the longest wingspan of any living bird, up to 3 metres (10 feet). The wingspan allows it to glide on ocean winds for hours without flapping its wings.

Fun Fact

Hummingbirds are the only birds that can hover in the air by flapping their wings in a figure-eight pattern, allowing them precise control over their position.

THE EVASIVE PEREGRINE FALCON

The peregrine falcon is the world's fastest bird. It is capable of diving at speeds over 320 kilometres per hour (200 Miles per hour) in a hunting stoop to catch prey in mid-air.

THE NIGHT SINGER: NIGHTINGALE

Nightingales are famous for their powerful and beautiful songs that can be heard during the night. They are symbols of love, melody, and the coming of spring.

THE RESOURCEFUL MACAW

Macaws use their powerful beaks not only to crack nuts and seeds, but also as a 'third foot' for climbing up trees. They are highly social and intelligent birds, known for their vibrant plumage and loud calls

MIGRATORY MARVELS: ARCTIC TERNS

Arctic terns experience two summers each year by migrating from the Arctic to the Antarctic and back again. They cover a distance of over 30,000, the longest migration of any animal.

DESERT DWELLERS

CAMELS: THE SHIPS OF THE DESERT

Camels are remarkably adapted to life in harsh desert environments. Camels are ideal for desert travellers due to their ability to go weeks without water and their sand-shielding eyelashes.

Fun Fact

The kangaroo rat in North American deserts can survive its entire life without drinking a single drop of water. Instead, it obtains the necessary water from the seeds it consumes.

FENNEC FOX: THE DESERT LISTENER

The fennec fox, native to the Sahara Desert, has unusually large ears. They serve two main purposes: dissipating heat and detecting prey moving underground.

THE RESILIENT DESERT TORTOISE

Desert tortoises can live in areas where ground temperatures exceed 60 degrees Celsius (140 degrees Fahrenheit). They survive by burrowing underground and can live up to 80 years.

THE VENOMOUS SCORPION

Scorpions, with their menacing curved tail, are desert survivors. They can control their metabolism to an extreme degree. It allows them to consume food only once a year if necessary.

THE MIGHTY MEERKAT

Meerkats are social animals, living in large groups in the deserts of Africa. Known for standing on their rear legs, they maintain a vigilant watch for predators while others forage or play.

JUNGLE JOURNEYS

THE STEALTHY JAGUARS

Jaguars are top predators in the tropical rainforests of South and Central America. Their powerful jaws and muscular build allow them to prey on other large mammals, sometimes even caimans and anacondas.

Fun Fact

A group of tigers is known as an 'ambush' or 'streak.' It reflects their exceptional skills in stealth and hunting.

THE PLAYFUL CAPUCHIN MONKEY

Capuchin monkeys utilise tools such as rocks for cracking nuts and sticks for foraging or insect capture. They are quick learners and often mimic human activities when observed.

THE COLOURFUL TOUCAN

Toucans are recognised for their large, colourful bills, which make up nearly half of their body length. Despite their size, these bills are surprisingly light because of a hollow structure.

THE SLOTH: SLOW AND STEADY

Sloths spend most of their lives hanging upside down from trees. A slow metabolism dictates their sluggish movement and low food intake, enabling energy conservation in their leafy habitat.

THE POISON DART FROG

These brightly coloured frogs are found in the Central and South American rainforests. Their vivid colours warn predators of their toxicity. Interestingly, they derive their poison from their diet of ants, centipedes, and mites.

MOUNTAIN MAJESTY

THE MAJESTIC SNOW LEOPARD

Snow leopards are native to the mountain ranges of Central and South Asia. They have thick fur and wide, fur-covered feet that act as natural snowshoes.

Fun Fact

The yak is a long-haired bovid. It is found throughout the Himalayan region of South Asia, the Tibetan Plateau, and as far north as Mongolia and Russia.

THE HIMALAYAN TAHR

Tahr, native to the rugged, wooded hills and mountain slopes of the Himalayas, are agile climbers. Their small, sturdy hooves allow them to effectively grip both smooth and rough surfaces.

THE MIGHTY MOUNTAIN GORILLA

Mountain gorillas live in the forests of Central Africa, at elevations of up to 8,000 to 13,000 feet. They have thicker fur compared to other great apes. It helps them survive in a habitat where temperatures often drop below freezing.

THE ANDEAN CONDOR

Soaring high in the sky, the Andean condor has the largest wingspan of any land bird, up to 3.3 metres (10 feet). This scavenger plays a crucial role in its ecosystem by cleaning up after dead animals.

THE ALPINE IBEX

Alpine ibexes are famous for climbing steep mountain terrain. Their rubber-like hooves, with a hard outer rim and soft centre, provide the grip needed for mountainous cliff.

GRASSLAND GALLIVANTS

THE RESOURCEFUL PRAIRIE DOG

Prairie dogs are native to the grasslands of North America. They are known for their complex underground burrows called 'towns'. Prairie dogs are very vocal creatures with a highly sophisticated vocal language. Not only do they make high-pitched yips and barks to warn about the presence of predators, but they also have different warning calls.

Fun Fact

The termite mounds found in African grasslands can be so large that they are visible from space.

THE ANTELOPE'S AGILITY

Antelopes are renowned for their agility and speed, which they use to evade predators on the African savannahs. Some species can reach speeds of up to 61 kilometres per hour (38 miles per hour) and make astonishing leaps over tall grass.

THE MIGRATORY WILDEBEEST

Wildebeest undertakes one of the most famous mass terrestrial migrations on Earth. Each year, over 1.5 million wildebeest travel over 3,000 kilometres (1,800 miles) in search of fresh grazing and water.

THE CUNNING COYOTE

The Coyote, often featured in Native American folklore as a trickster, is a highly adaptable predator found throughout North and Central America. They can change their breeding habits and diet to suit their environment.

THE REGAL SECRETARY BIRD

The Secretary bird is distinctive for its long legs and an eagle-like body. This bird of prey hunts on foot, stomping its prey to death with powerful strikes of its feet.

RIVERINE REFLECTIONS

THE ENIGMATIC PLATYPUS

One of nature's most unusual animals, the platypus is a mammal that lays eggs. It has a duck-like bill and webbed feet. It is one of the few venomous mammals, with males carrying venom potent enough to cause severe pain to humans.

THE INDUSTRIOUS BEAVER

Beavers are nature's engineers. Their dam-building activities can transform landscapes, creating ecosystems that support diverse wildlife. They use their strong teeth to cut down trees and shrubs for their construction.

Fun Fact

A group of otters is charmingly called a 'romps,' reflecting their playful nature.

THE PROLIFIC PIRANHA

Piranhas are native to South American rivers. They are known for their sharp teeth and a reputed ability to devour large animals quickly. However, they primarily feed on fish and scavenge on animal remains.

THE GRACEFUL SWAN

Swans are symbols of elegance and grace. Known for their lifelong monogamous relationships, they use synchronised swimming and mutual preening to strengthen their bonds.

THE AGILE OTTER

Otters are playful river dwellers who are excellent swimmers. They can close their ears and nostrils underwater. They use rocks as tools to crack open shellfish, which is a key part of their diet.

ARCTIC ANTICS

Fun Fact

Did you know that reindeer eyes change colour through the seasons? Their eyes change from gold in summer to blue in winter, adapting to varying light levels for improved vision.

THE SLEEK ARCTIC FOX

Arctic foxes seasonally change fur colour for camouflage: white to blend with snow, brown or grey for tundra's rocks and plants.

THE HARDY POLAR BEAR

Polar bears are the largest land carnivores, and their bodies are adapted to the cold Arctic environment. They have black skin under their translucent fur which helps them absorb heat from the sun.

THE SOCIABLE BELUGA

Belugas are known for their distinct white colour and vocal behaviour. They are sometimes called 'canaries of the sea' because of their wide range of sounds.

THE MYSTERIOUS NARWHAL

Narwhals are often called the 'unicorns of the sea.' They have a large tusk from a protruding canine tooth. They inhabit Arctic waters and their tusks are believed to have sensory capabilities.

THE MAJESTIC WALRUS

Walruses are easily recognisable by their long tusks, which can grow up to a metre in length. These tusks are used for fighting, dominance, and digging ice or hauling themselves out of the water.

ISLAND INHABITANTS

THE ELUSIVE MADAGASCAR LEMUR

Lemurs are native only to Madagascar. They are known for their wide, reflective eyes and long, bushy tails. They play a crucial role in their ecosystems as seed dispersers and pollinators.

Fun Fact

Dodo birds, now extinct, were flightless birds that lived on the islands of Mauritius. They were about 1 metre tall and weighed about 20 kilograms.

THE FLIGHTLESS KIWI

The Kiwi, New Zealand's iconic bird, is unusual among birds because it has nostrils at the end of its beak. Kiwis are flightless, nocturnal birds that lay remarkably large eggs for their size.

THE MAJESTIC GALÁPAGOS TORTOISE

These giant tortoises can live for more than 100 years. They are among the largest tortoises in the world. They have evolved different shell shapes depending on their island's environment.

THE COLOURFUL HAWAIIAN HONEYCREEPER

Hawaiian honeycreepers are known for their vibrant plumage and diverse beak shapes, They have evolved to exploit different ecological niches.

THE FIERCE KOMODO DRAGON

The Komodo dragon, native to Indonesia's Komodo Island, is the largest living species of lizard, reaching lengths of 3 metres and weights over 70 kilograms.

URBAN ADAPTERS

Fun Fact

Crows have been observed using a clever technique to crack nuts: placing them on roads and allowing passing cars to crush them.

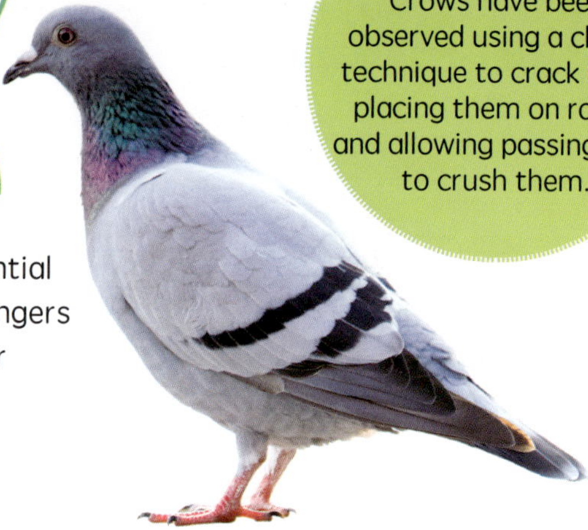

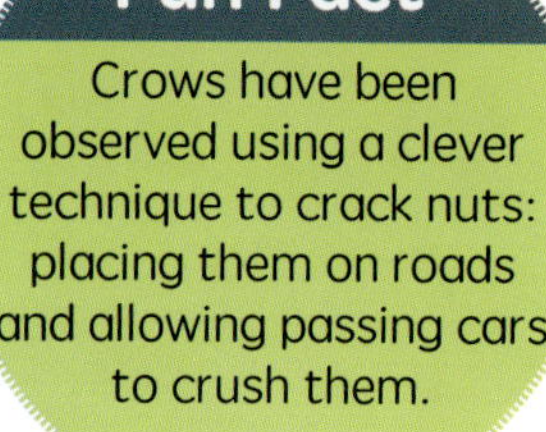

THE PIGEON POST

Pigeons, often seen as the quintessential urban bird, were once used as messengers during wars. They are known for their exceptional navigation abilities.

THE RESOURCEFUL RACCOON

Raccoons have adapted well to urban environments. They use their dexterous front paws and high intelligence to open doors and access food in trash cans.

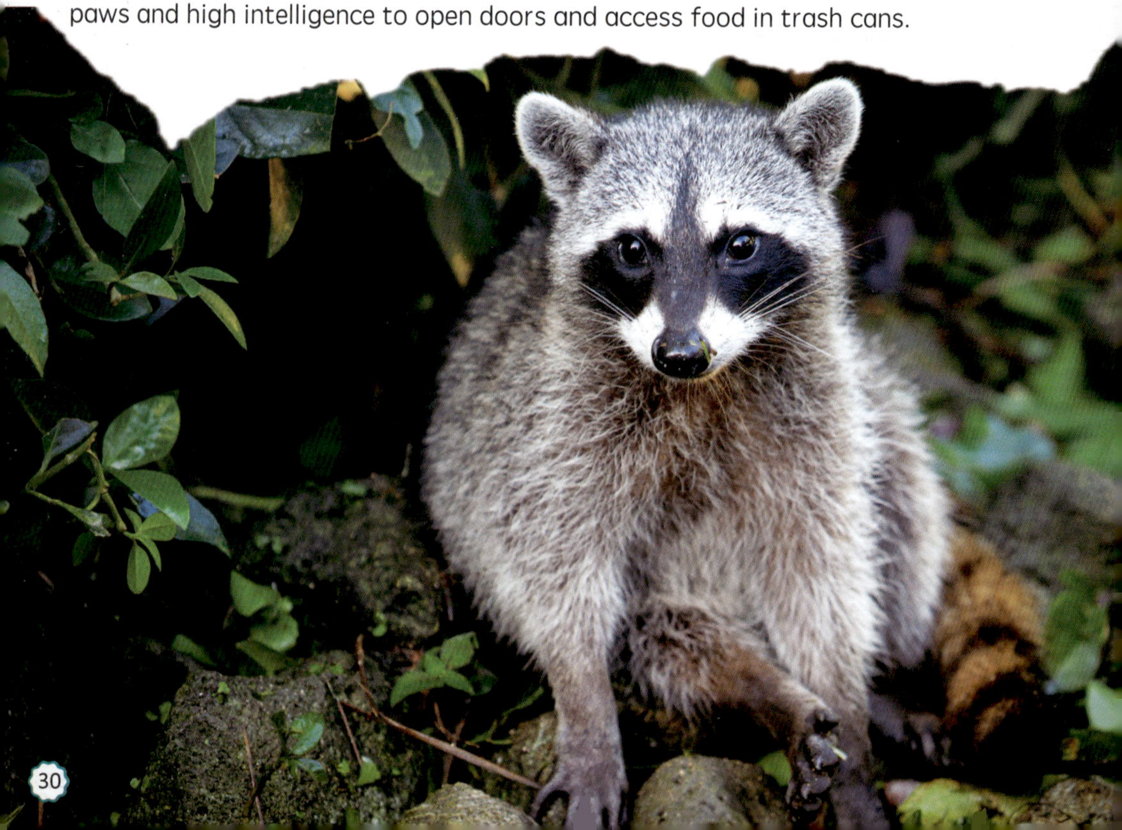

THE ADAPTIVE FOX

Urban foxes are becoming increasingly common in cities. They adapt to urban living by scavenging food from bins and gardens.

THE CUNNING CROW

Crows are among the most intelligent birds, capable of using tools and solving complex problems. They thrive in urban areas by manipulating their environment to get food.

THE SURVIVING SQUIRREL

Grey squirrels often thrive in urban parks and gardens. They are agile and quick. They have adapted to a wide variety of habitats by storing food and adjusting their diet based on availability.

UNDERGROUND UNVEILED

Fun Fact

Badgers create setts, their elaborate burrows, which can be centuries old. They provide homes for successive generations, showcasing their remarkable digging skills.

THE BURROWING MOLE

Moles spend most of their lives underground. They use their powerful forelimbs to dig complex tunnel systems. These tunnels help them hunt their primary food source, earthworms.

THE INGENIOUS EARTHWORM

Earthworms play a critical role in aerating the soil. They break down dead organic material, enhancing soil fertility and helping plants grow.

THE FUNGAL FARMER: LEAF-CUTTER ANTS

Famous for their unique agricultural practices, leaf-cutter ants cut leaves and bring them to their underground nests. There, they cultivate the fungi that serve as their main food supply.

THE SUBTERRANEAN ANT QUEEN

The queen ant, residing deep underground, ensures colony growth by laying thousands of eggs.

THE MYSTERIOUS BLIND SALAMANDER

Blind salamanders live in dark caves. They have adapted to their environment by losing their sight and developing enhanced other senses, such as sensitivity to water currents and vibrations.

NOCTURNAL NIGHTS

THE MYSTICAL BARN OWL

Barn owls, known for their heart-shaped faces, have exceptional hearing. They have their ears placed asymmetrically for precise vertical and horizontal sound locations. This adaptation allows them to hunt small mammals in the dark.

Fun Fact

Aye-ayes, a lemur species, use their elongated middle finger to tap trees for grubs. Then, they chew holes and extract them with the same digit.

THE ELUSIVE NIGHTJAR

Nightjars are nocturnal birds with camouflaged plumage that makes them nearly invisible in woodland habitats during the day. At night, they come alive, hunting insects with their wide mouths.

THE AGILE OPOSSUM

Opossums are North America's only marsupial. They often feign death when threatened, a behaviour known as 'playing possum,' which can deter predators.

THE ECHOING BAT

Bats are masters of the night, using echolocation to navigate and hunt in complete darkness. They use high-frequency sounds and echo analysis to precisely locate prey, making them crucial for insect population control.

THE SILENT HEDGEHOG

Hedgehogs are nocturnal animals known for their spiny protection. When threatened, they roll into a tight ball, allowing the spines to shield them from predators.

FOREST FORAGERS

THE DILIGENT WOODPECKER

Woodpeckers are equipped with shock-absorbent heads that prevent brain damage while they peck at wood to find insects or create nesting sites. Their long tongues can extend far to extract insects from crevices.

Fun Fact

With cheek pouches that can expand to three times their head size, chipmunks efficiently transport food to their burrows.

THE WATCHFUL DEER

Deer have highly developed senses of hearing and smell, which alert them to the presence of predators. They can also move silently through dense forests due to their light footedness.

THE SCURRYING SQUIRREL

Tree squirrels are expert climbers and jumpers. They have strong hind legs and bushy tails for balance. They collect and store nuts for winter, showing an impressive memory of where they hide their food.

THE PROTECTIVE PORCUPINE

As a defense, porcupines use quills, sharp spines that easily detach and embed in attackers, effectively deterring them.

THE VERSATILE RACCOON

Raccoons are adept at manipulating their environment to access food. They use their dexterous paws to open jars, doors, and trash cans. They are omnivorous, eating anything from fruits to small animals.

SAVANNAH SOJOURNERS

THE STATELY GIRAFFE

Giraffes are the tallest mammals on Earth, with necks that allow them to reach leaves high up in trees. Their height also provides an advantage in spotting predators from afar.

THE POWERFUL LION

Lions are known as the 'kings of the jungle,' but they actually live in grasslands and savannas. Unlike other cats, lions form complex social groups known as prides. They are matriarchal societies primarily dominated by female lions.

Fun Fact

African elephants have ears shaped like the African continent, while Asian elephants have smaller, rounder ears resembling the Indian subcontinent.

THE HARDY WARTHOG

Warthogs use their long, curved tusks to dig and for defense. They are known for kneeling on their padded knees while foraging with their muscular snouts.

THE ZEALOUS ZEBRA

Zebras have distinctive black-and-white stripes that are unique to each individual, much like human fingerprints. These stripes may serve multiple purposes, including camouflage, heat management, and deterring flies.

THE ENDURING ELEPHANT

African elephants are essential to their habitats. They help to maintain forest and savannah ecosystems. Their movements, across the land, create pathways for other animals and help in seed dispersal.

COASTAL CREATURES

Fun Fact

Seahorses are the only creatures where the male bears the unborn young. Male seahorses have a pouch on their stomach in which to carry babies, up to 2,000 at a time.

THE CRAFTY CRAB

Crabs are equipped with a pair of pincers that serve both as a tool for hunting and as a defence against predators. They can also regenerate lost limbs, enhancing their survival chances in hostile environments.

THE RESILIENT SEA TURTLE

Sea turtles are ancient mariners of the ocean, known for their long migrations between feeding grounds and the beaches where they were born. They return to the same nesting sites every few years to lay their eggs.

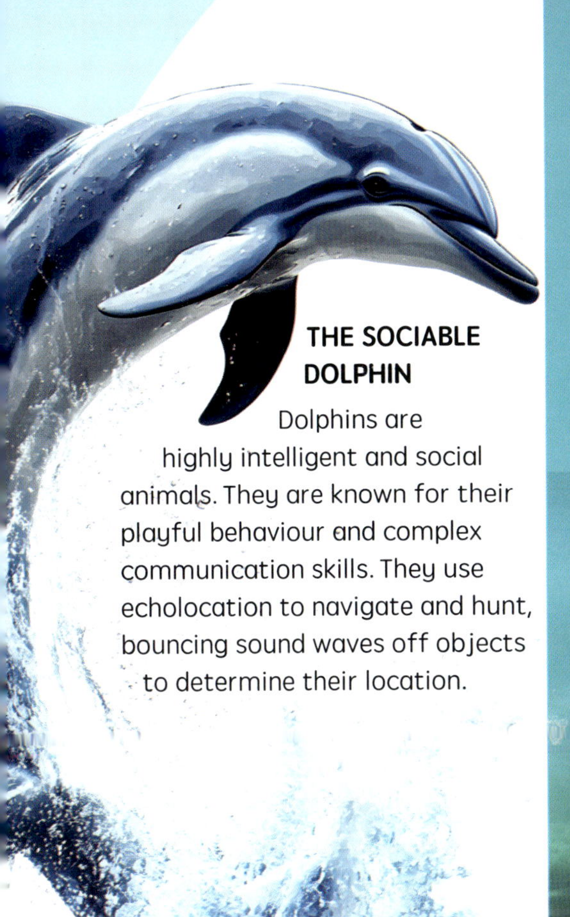

THE SOCIABLE DOLPHIN

Dolphins are highly intelligent and social animals. They are known for their playful behaviour and complex communication skills. They use echolocation to navigate and hunt, bouncing sound waves off objects to determine their location.

THE MYSTERIOUS MANATEE

Manatees, often called sea cows, are gentle giants that graze on sea grasses in shallow coastal waters. Despite their size, they are graceful swimmers. They use their powerful tails to propel themselves through the water.

THE PERSISTENT LIMPET

Limpets are small marine creatures. They cling tenaciously to rocky shores, withstanding crashing waves. By grazing on algae, they prevent overgrowth and maintain balance in intertidal zones. They play a small but vital role in coastal ecosystems.

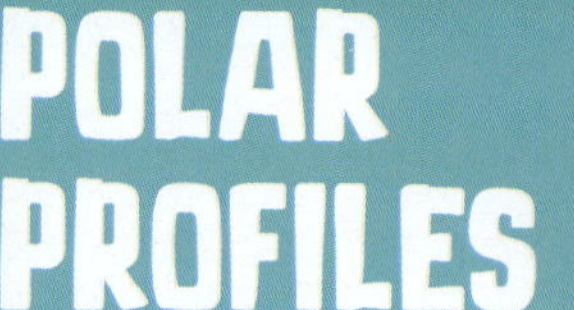

POLAR PROFILES

THE TENACIOUS MUSK OX

Musk oxen have thick coats and a strong smell. They use their smell to mark territory and attract mates. They form defensive circles with their young in the middle when threatened by predators.

THE EMPEROR PENGUIN

Emperor penguins are the tallest and heaviest of all penguin species. They are the only animals to breed during the Antarctic winter. They huddle together to escape the extreme cold, taking turns moving to the group's warm centre.

THE SNOWY OWL

Snowy owls are adapted to live in the Arctic tundra, with their white feathers providing camouflage against the snow. They have keen eyesight and hearing. These are crucial for hunting in their dimly lit habitats.

SNOW KINGS: THE ARCTIC WOLVES

Arctic wolves, isolated from other wolf species, are smaller and whiter than their relatives. They can survive temperatures as low as –50°C (–58°F).

THE ARCTIC HARE

Arctic hares survive in extremely cold climates by having shortened ears, thick fur, and a high-fat diet. They can run up to 60 kilometres per hour (40 Miles per hour) to escape predators.

WHAT'S HAPPENING TODAY?

A WORLD IN DANGER

Today, many animals and plants are disappearing faster than ever before. Scientists call this a 'mass extinction,' which means many species are going extinct in a short time. This is happening because of things like deforestation, pollution, and climate change. We need to protect these living things so they don't disappear forever.

LOSING HOMES

One big reason animals and plants are disappearing is because they are losing their homes. As more people need space for houses, farms, and roads, natural places like forests and wetlands are being destroyed. Without their homes, many species can't survive.

HUNTING

Another problem is that some animals are hunted for food or to be kept as trophies. Some people capture animals and plants to sell, which can make it hard for these species to survive in the wild.

THE VANISHING RIVER DOLPHIN

In China, there was a special dolphin called the baiji that lived in the Yangtze River. Sadly, because of pollution, fishing, and other problems, the baiji hasn't been seen for many years and is now considered extinct. This shows how important it is to protect animals and their homes before it's too late.

Fun Fact

Every day, many species, especially insects and small creatures in tropical forests, go extinct.

ON THE BRINK

THE RED LIST GROWS

Every year, scientists check which animals and plants are in danger of disappearing forever. These species are put on a special list called the International Union for Conservation of Nature (IUCN) Red List. Sadly, this list keeps growing. More and more animals and plants are becoming rare, and if we don't help, they may be gone one day.

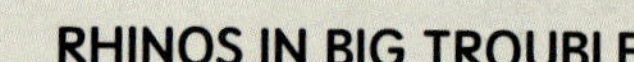

RHINOS IN BIG TROUBLE

Rhinos are one of the most endangered animals in the world. There are only five kinds of rhinos, and all of them are in danger. Some, like the Javan, Sumatran, and black rhinos, are critically endangered, meaning there are very few left. People hunt them for their horns, and their homes are disappearing. If we don't protect them, we might lose these giant, gentle creatures forever!

THE DISAPPEARING FROGS

Frogs, toads, and salamanders belong to a big group called amphibians. More than half of them are in danger. One big reason is a deadly fungus disease called chytrid, which makes them very sick. Some frogs, like the gastric-brooding frog of Australia, are already gone forever. This frog was special because it swallowed its eggs and let the tadpoles grow inside its stomach. Sadly, it disappeared in the 1980s.

CORAL REEFS IN DANGER

Coral reefs are colourful underwater homes for many sea animals. But these beautiful reefs could disappear in the next 100–200 years! Pollution, global warming, and changes in the ocean make life hard for coral. If reefs disappear, many fish and sea creatures will lose their homes. That is why it is important to keep our oceans clean and safe.

Titles in this Series

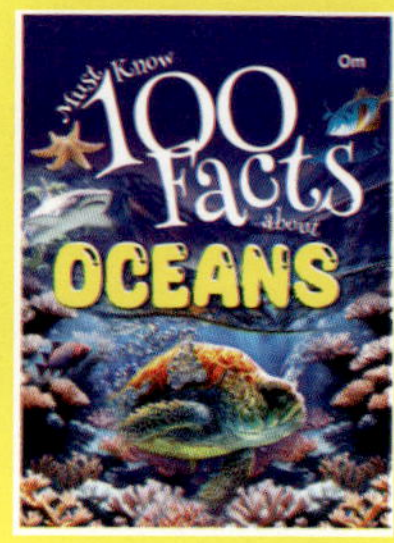

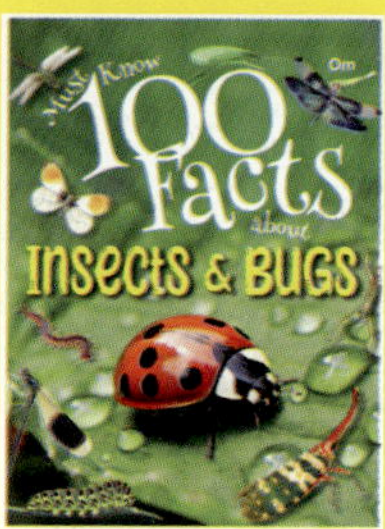

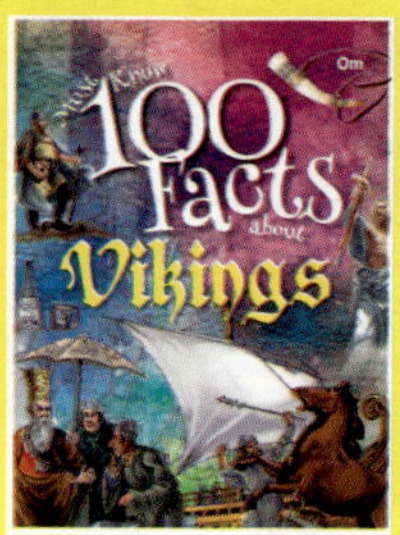

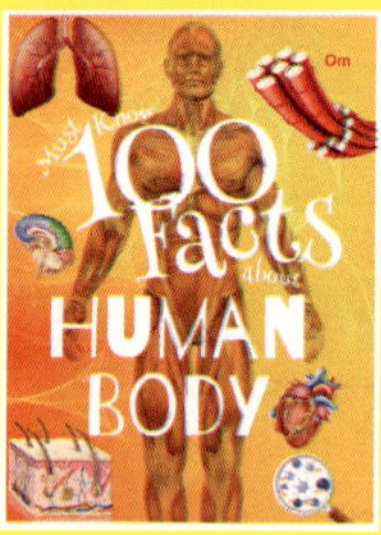

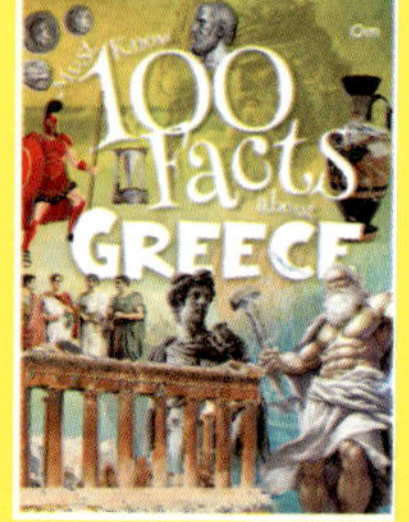

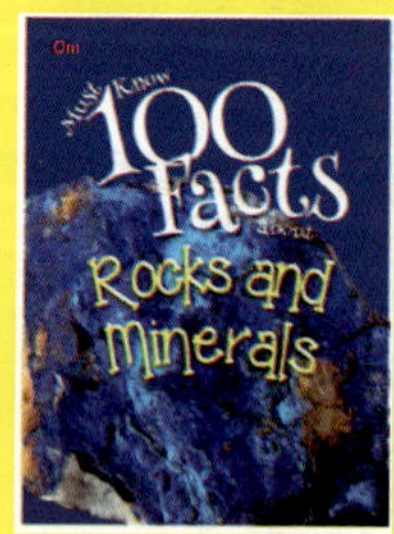